What's in this book ☞

oh, and a glossary/index

Cognitive Psychology

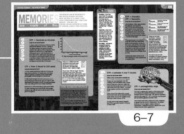

6–7

8–9

10–12

12–13

MEMORIES
are made of this

OUR MEMORY CAN BE REPRESENTED AND STUDIED IN MANY DIFFERENT WAYS. ONE WAY IS TO DIVIDE IT INTO SHORT-TERM MEMORY AND LONG-TERM MEMORY – STM AND LTM.
STM AND LTM ARE DIFFERENT IN TERMS OF DURATION, CAPACITY AND ENCODING.

duration

STM → Seconds or minutes

How do we know this?

A classic study by Peterson & Peterson (1959) assessed the duration of STM. A group of 24 college students were given *consonant syllables* (also called *nonsense trigrams*). Each trigram was followed by a 3 digit number. Participants had to count backwards in 3s from that number until told to stop and recall the trigram. In general participants had 100% recall when stopped within 3 seconds but this dropped to almost no one being able to recall the trigram correctly after 18 seconds.

▲ Graph showing the results of this experiment

LTM → From 2 hours to 100 years

How do we know this?

A clever natural experiment made use of American high school yearbooks. For many years it has been common practice to publish a book of individual photographs of all the people in a school year.

A team of psychologists showed these yearbooks to about 400 people between the ages of 17 and 74, and asked them to put names to faces. For each participant only some of the photos were of their classmates.

Bahrick *et al.* (1975) found that people tested within 15 years of leaving school were about 90% accurate in their recall. After 48 years recall was about 70% for photo recognition.

Nairne *et al.* (1999) found that participants could recall nouns flashed on a screen for up to 96 seconds. The nouns were between 4 and 7 letters in length.

Why did their STM last longer? This time participants were shown items-to-be-remembered and then, when asked to recall them, they were again shown the items and just had to put them in the correct order. The loss of information from STM is much less drastic when a purer measure of recall is used.

HOW SCIENCE WORKS

One criticism that is made about this research is that the studies lack validity. Psychologists are only studying one kind of memory – memory for syllables and words – whereas much of the time our memories are concerned with other things, such as what I did last night or what my children look like.

On the other hand there are times when we are remembering words – like ordering drinks in a pub or remembering someone's phone number.

Duration– How long does it last? For example when you meet someone, how long can you remember their name? This is the duration of the memory. You might say *'It depends if I repeat it over and over'* – indeed it does.

Capacity– How much can you remember at any one time? If I read out a list of 20 numbers and then ask you to tell me what they were, you will only remember some of them – your STM has a limited capacity.

Encoding– Information is stored in memory in different forms, for example you might remember someone's name – this is a verbal or acoustic form of encoding. Or you might remember what they look like. This is a visual encoding.

encoding

STM → Acoustic
LTM → Semantic

How do we know this?

Alan Baddeley (1966) demonstrated the different ways that STM and LTM are encoded by giving participants various word lists to memorise. In one list the words all sounded the same (acoustically similar), in another list they meant the same thing (semantically similar) – see lists on the right.

When participants were asked to recall the words they were shown all the words and had to decide on the correct order. If they were asked to do this immediately (STM recall) they didn't do well with acoustically similar words, which suggests that words are stored in an acoustic form in STM.

Semantically similar words posed little difficulty for STM recall but led to mudded LTM.

List A acoustically similar	cat, cab, can, cad,mad, max, mat, man, map
List B acoustically dissimilar	pit, few, cow, pen, sup, bar, day, hot, rig, bun
List C semantically similar	great, large, big, huge, broad, long, tall, fat, wide, high
List D semantically dissimilar	good, huge, hot, safe, thin, deep, strong, foul, old, late

Things are not quite that simple – it seems that visual codes may sometimes be used in STM. For example when participants were shown pictures (a visual task) and prevented from performing verbal rehearsal (they had to say *'la la la'*), then they did use visual codes (Brandimote et al., 1992).

The same is true for LTM – sometimes it is related to visual or acoustic codes (Frost, 1972, and Nelson and Rothbart, 1972).

capacity

STM → between 4 and 7 chunks

How do we know this?

Miller (1956) was the first to identify the limit of STM, claiming it was 7 ± 2 items. People can cope reasonably well with counting seven dots flashed onto a screen but not many more than this. Miller also found that that people can recall 5 *words* as well as they can recall 5 *letters* – we *chunk* things together and then can remember more.

Other research has refined this concept. First of all it seems we can remember more small chunks (such as one-syllable words) than large chunks (Simon, 1974).

Second, more recent research suggests that STM is generally limited to 4 chunks (Cowan, 2001).

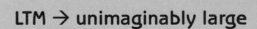

LTM → unimaginably large

How can we know this?

One way to estimate the capacity of the human brain is to estimate the number of synapses (connections between neurons) in the brain - the capacity of memory may be in the range 10^{13}–10^{15}, or between one thousand and one million gigabytes (Merkle, 1988).

This sounds small when compared to most computers. It appears that the secret is organisation. The human brain has evolved a highly complex system of organisation. Computers may have capacity but, as yet, cannot rival the brain's organisation.

Maintenance
Rehearsal

Environmental
stimuli → **SENSORY MEMORY SM** → Attention → **SHORT-TERM MEMORY STM** ⇄ Retrieval / Elaborative Rehearsal → **LONG-TERM MEMORY LTM**

Information retrieval

MULTI-STORE MODEL MSM

Atkinson and Shiffrin (1968, 197

SENSORY MEMORY

The eyes, ears, nose, fingers etc.

These stores constantly receive large amounts of information.

Information remains in the store for a very brief period.

Most information receives no attention.

Demonstrated by Sperling (1960)

Participants were shown 12 digits/letters in 3 rows, as below. Exposure lasted 50 milliseconds. If they were asked to recall all 12 items recall was about 42%. If they were told immediately afterwards to just recall one row, recall was 75%. This shows that information in sensory memory disappears very quickly.

| 7 1 V F |
| X L 5 3 |
| B 4 W 7 |

SHORT-TERM MEMORY

Limited duration (seconds/minutes).

Limited capacity (about 4 chunks).

Mainly acoustic encoding

LONG-TERM MEMORY

Long duration (hours and years).

Large capacity.

Mainly semantic encoding

Demonstrated by brain scans

The prefrontal cortex is active when a person is working on STM tasks (Beardsley, 1997).

The hippocampus is active when LTM is used (Squire *et al.* 1992).

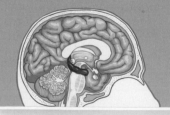

MAINTENANCE REHEARSAL

Verbal – repeating something over and over again.

ELABORATIVE REHEARSAL

Deeper processing of material, for example, considering its meaning.

Demonstrated by Craik and Lockhart (1972)

Participants read a list of words and were asked questions about each, such as

(1) 'Is the word printed in capital letters?' (shallow processing).

(2) 'Does the word rhyme with 'train'? (phonemic processing).

(3) 'Is the word a type of fruit?' (deeper, semantic processing).

Those words that were semantically processed were more likely to be remembered. This demonstrates the importance of elaborative processing for LTM.

Structure & Process

The model provides an account of both the structure of memory and the processes that enable information to be transferred between memory stores.

A young man, KF, was injured in a motorcycle accident. His STM was affected – but only his ability to deal with verbal information. He could still process visual information normally in STM.

STM is not just one store

LOTS OF EVIDENCE SUPPORTS SEPARATE STORES

Brain scans suggest that there are separate stores for STM and LTM. This is further supported by case studies of individuals with brain damage, such as HM.

HM suffered from severe epilepsy which originated in the hippocampal region, so the doctors removed his hippocampi. After the operation HM's personality and intellect remained intact as did his STM (he could remember things for a few seconds). However he could no longer form new long-term memories though he could remember things from a long time ago.

This suggests that the hippocampus may function as a memory 'gateway' through which new memories must pass before entering permanent storage in the brain.

LTM is not just one store

The MSM suggests that LTM is just one store whereas evidence from studies of people with brain damage indicates a number of different LTM stores, for example:

Semantic memory refers to the memory of meanings, understandings, and other concept-based knowledge unrelated to specific experiences

Episodic memory refers to the memory for events – what you did last week or what you watched on TV last night.

Procedural memory refers to the memory for knowing how to do things, like ride a bicycle or being able to read.

Are STM and LTM separate?

Consider this experiment: Participants are given a list of letters to learn. The list is either
RTH JWP MQN ZRT or
AQA BBC ITV GPO.
The second set of letters is much easier to remember because the chunks should be meaningful. But where does the meaning come from? You have to access LTM to perform this task. Which means that STM and LTM are not as separate as the MSM model suggests

Ruchkin *et al.* (2003) demonstrated this in an experiment using words and pseudowords (words that sound like real words but have no meaning). While participants learned the words their brain activity was watched. Processing the real words involved much more brain activity than when the pseudowords were processed. Ruchkin *et al.* concluded that STM is just a part of LTM.

MSM has clear predictions which encourage empirical testing.

Empirical testing is important in order to establish whether a theory (or model) is correct. 'Empirical' refers to gaining direct experience as opposed to presenting a rational argument.

HOW SCIENCE WORKS

The studies that have been used to support the MSM have been accused of lacking validity. For one thing such studies often involve college students who may have superior memories and therefore the findings should not be generalised.

Also the studies are usually concerned with one particular sort of memory (semantic memory) and tell us little about other kinds of memory.

Finally the studies are conducted in labs which may create demand characteristics so that participants' behaviour is not 'normal'

On the other hand lab studies can be well-controlled so that the findings may be more reliable.

EVALUATION

WORKING MEMORY MODEL

Working memory is concerned with the temporary storage and manipulation of information. It operates over only a few seconds.

The central executive has no storage capacity except for the small amount necessary to allocate incoming information to resources.

Central executive

I supervise the working memory and decide which of my slave systems should deal with incoming information.

Episodic buffer

The episodic buffer provides temporary storage. It is like a TV screen that can hold information which is limited in capacity and needs refreshing. However, unlike the TV it is multidimensional and represents not only visual and acoustic information but possibly also smell and taste. Besides being temporary storage it also allows information to move to and from long-term memory.

EVALUATION

Dual task performance

Hitch and Baddeley (1976) demonstrated that when participants performed two STM tasks using the same modality (i.e. both phonological) slowed performance slowed, whereas two tasks using different modalities (i.e. visual and phonological tasks) did not affect each other. This shows that WM must have separate modalities.

Brain scans

Bunge *et al.* (2000) showed there was more activity in the brain when participants were doing tasks simultaneously than one after the other, which supports the involvement of a central executive.

When people are processing sounds, two different areas of the brain are active, supporting the separate components of the phonological system (Baddeley, 1982).

Slave system – phonological (sound) loop

Phonological store
Inner ear

Articulatory process
Inner voice

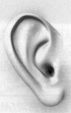

The 'inner ear' remembers speech sounds. The 'inner voice' repeats any verbal input in a loop of about two seconds' duration to prevent it from decaying. The phonological loop may play a key role in the acquisition of vocabulary, particularly in the early childhood years

Slave system – visuo-spatial sketchpad

Visual cache
A passive store

Inner scribe
Rehearses information

Logie (1995) suggested that the visuo-spatial sketchpad could be divided into two further subsystems.
The visual cache holds information about form and colour.
The inner scribe deals with spatial and movement information.

Try this

How many windows are there in your house?

In order to work out the number of windows you probably had a picture of your house in your working memory and used the visuo-spatial sketchpad to count the number of windows.

Phonological loop

Baddeley *et al*. (1975) showed that people have more difficulty remembering long words than short words (the word length effect) presumably because the phonological loop only holds about 2 seconds-worth of information.

Brain-damaged patients

Shallice and Warrington (1970) studied KF whose LTM was intact and in STM he could cope reasonably well with visual information and meaningful sounds but not verbal material. This suggests that only his phonological loop was affected.

Another patient, LH (studied by Farah *et al*., 1988), performed better on spatial tasks rather than those involving visual imagery, which suggests separate visual and spatial systems.

strengths

The model makes predictions that can be tested empirically and thus permits the model to be supported or refuted.

It offers a further development of the MSM which proposed that memory was not one activity but several different stores; the WMM further distinguished these stores.

weaknesses

Some of the components are unsatisfactorily explained. For example the central executive is seen as equivalent to 'attention' but it is not clear how this operates or could be tested.

The WMM is limited to working (short-term) memory and says nothing about LTM.

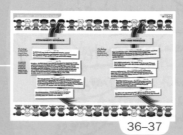

Developmental Psychology

Bowlby's theory (see page 24) suggests that disruption of attachment in early life is likely to have a negative effect on social and emotional development.

DISRUPTION

There is one major problem with studies of children who have experienced disruption of attachment – it is difficult to separate the effects of physical and emotional disruption. A child who is physically separated from their primary attachment figure may also experience disruption of emotional care (because no substitute care is available). Therefore we cannot be sure whether any ill effects are due to physical or emotional disruption.

In fact emotional disruption can occur even when a mother is physically present. For example, people with depression are physically present but often unable to provide emotional care.

HOW SCIENCE WORKS

The studies by James and Joyce Robertson were **case studies** of unique individuals and situations, which means they may lack generalisability. On the other hand, these case studies provide a lot of rich detail which has allowed people to gain important insights into the behaviour of young children.

Other research discussed on this page has used quite large samples but faces other problems. For ethical reasons it is not possible to artificially create situations where children are separated from their mothers. Therefore research relies on natural experiments and observations where it may be difficult to disentangle important variables such as physical versus emotional disruption. This makes it difficult to demonstrate that disruption has been the cause of subsequent developmental difficulties.

Jargon watch

On this page we are concerned with the effects of **disruption of attachment** on children's emotional development. On the next spread we will look at **failure to form an attachment** in early life. Disruption may be for hours, weeks, months or years. The key point is that the child has experienced a break in their relationship with their primary attachment figure but they have formed attachments.

Physical and emotional disruption

In the 1950s James and Joyce Robertson filmed a number of children in 'brief separation' – they were separated from their mothers for brief periods. One film was of Laura, aged 2, who was in hospital for two weeks. In the 1950s, when the film was made, parents were only allowed short visits with children in hospital so Laura was on her own much of the time. The nurses provided excellent physical care but little emotional support. In the film you can see that Laura is very withdrawn and depressed.

Before the Robertsons presented their films, a number of studies had indicated that disruption of attachment may lead to depression. In one classic study Spitz and Wolf (1946) drew attention to a group of about 100 children who were in long-term hospital because their parents had died during the bombing of London in World War II. They coined the term 'anaclitic depression' to describe the children who were severely withdrawn and apathetic, and whose physical, social and intellectual development was impaired. They explained anaclitic depression as a form of depression that arises following separation from a loving mother or mother figure.

Physical disruption alone

The Robertsons also filmed four other children, all aged less than three years of age, who had been placed in foster care for a few weeks with the Robertsons while their mothers were in hospital. The Robertsons endeavoured to sustain a high level of substitute emotional care and keep routines similar to those at home. Fathers' visits were arranged regularly to maintain emotional links with home. Kate was taken to visit her mother in hospital and was much more settled after this. All the children seemed to adjust well.

Emotional disruption alone

A depressed mother is often emotionally unavailable. Hart et al. (1998) studied about 100 infants in the strange situation with their mothers. Infants whose mothers were classified as depressed showed less separation anxiety, less proximity to their mothers, and greater proximity to a stranger; all signs of insecure attachment.

Lyons-Ruth et al. (1986) found that infants of depressed mothers are more likely to exhibit slowed development and unstable, insecure-avoidant attachment behaviors.

Long-term vulnerability

There is considerable evidence that children who experience early disruption of attachment recover well if the disruption stops. For example Bohman and Sigvardsson (1979) studied over 600 adopted children many of whom, at the age of 11, were classified as 'problem children'. Ten years later, after successful adoptions, they were the same as 'normal' adults in terms of social and emotional development.

However for many children, such as those with depressed mothers, the disruptions continue throughout childhood and are associated with long-term effects.

Even amongst those who appear to recover there seems to be a long-term vulnerability to develop mental disorders if they encounter emotional difficulties later in life (the diathesis – stress model). This was shown in a study by Bifulco et al. (1992) involving over 200 women who had lost mothers through separation or death before they were 17. This group was twice as likely to suffer from depressive or anxiety disorders when the children became adults.

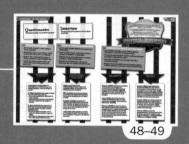

48–49

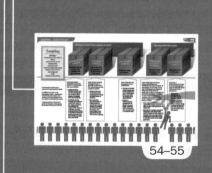

54–55

50–51

58–59

56–57

52–53

Research Methods

In a universe not so very far away...

Validity and reliability are the key concepts to consider when evaluating research.

Validity refers to the legitimacy or soundness of a measurement or study.

Validity

Internal validity

Whether a study or measurement has measured what it intended to measure.

External validity

The extent to which a research finding can be generalised beyond the research situation.

Mundane realism

The extent to which features of a research study mirror the 'real' world (everyday life).

Ecological validity

Concerns the research *setting* i.e. the environment in which the study was conducted, and whether we can generalise from this to other settings such as everyday life.

Experimental realism

The extent to which participants believe in the experimental set up and therefore will behave 'naturally'.

Population validity

Concerns the research *population*, i.e. the people used in the study, and whether we can generalise from them to other people.

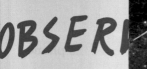

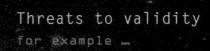

Threats to validity

for example ...

Contrived set-up
Demand characteristics
Extraneous variables
Social desirability
bias

(See glossary for
jargon busting)

Threats to reliability

for example ...

Ambiguous questions
on a questionnaire or
interview
Confusing behavioural
categories in
observations

Reliability
is about consistency – we
can rely on the results.

If you repeat the same study or test, you
should get the same outcome.

If a study lacks reliability then it
lacks validity.

Reliability

Pa...

In s...
obs...
oft...

Internal reliability

The extent to which something
(such as a questionnaire) is
consistent within itself. For a
questionnaire to have high
internal reliability, all questions
should be assessing the same
thing (or an aspect of it).

External reliability

The extent to which a
measure varies over time.
A questionnaire or interview
should produce the same result
each time it is used with the
same person.

Behaviour check

EXPO	explora
EXPS	explora
PLYO	playing
PLYS	playing
PASO	passiv
PASS	passiv
CONTO	physic
CONTS	physi
SBYO	stand
SBYS	stand

72–73

78–79

74–75

82–83

80–81

76–77

Biological Psychology

64–65

66–67

68–69

70–71

Daily hassles

Hassles are those frustrating, irritating everyday experiences that occur regularly in our work, home and personal life. For most of us, our life stressors are not major life events like divorce, redundancy or the death of a loved one but the relatively minor annoyances that affect us more regularly and which accumulate over time.

Research into hassles

Bouteyre *et al.* (2007) investigated the relationship between daily hassles and mental health in students undergoing the initial transition from school to university. After students completed a hassles questionnaire and a depression inventory, the researchers found that over 40% of the new students suffered from depressive symptoms and there was a positive correlation between scores on the hassles scale and the incidence of depressive symptoms.

Other research has shown that the effect of daily hassles tends to accumulate over the course of a day. Hassles that haven't been dealt with successfully at the time add to the impact of subsequent stressors. For example, Gulian *et al.* (1990), found that participants who had endured a stressful day at work reported higher levels of stress on their journey home.

In a study of nurses, Gervais (2005) found that although daily hassles increased job strain and decreased performance, these negative effects were, to some degree, offset by daily uplifts, i.e. the positive experiences of everyday life, such as receiving a compliment or a thank you from a patient.

Hassles versus life changes

Daily hassles are now accepted as being comparable to, if not greater than, life changes as a significant source of stress. An Australian study found that daily hassles were linked to greater psychological and physical dysfunction than major negative life events (Ruffin, 1993). However, the greater negative influence of daily hassles on our wellbeing may be due, in part, to the reduced social support received from others. People tend to rally round when a person is undergoing a major life event such as divorce or bereavement, but a broken iPod or missed bus just don't get the same reaction, regardless of how devastating you find these events!

Hassle headlines:

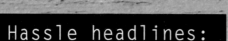

... argument with friends ... slow computer ... rude people ... traff

Why are hassles so stressful?

The accumulation effect – an accumulation of minor daily stressors creates persistent irritations, frustrations and overloads which then result in more serious stress reactions such as anxiety and depression.

The amplification effect – Chronic stress caused by negative life events may deplete a person's resources, making them more vulnerable to the influence of daily hassles.

Action theory – hassles are disruptive because they involve effort expenditure, which prevents us from pursuing our primary goals. This can include effort spent in problem solving how to deal with the hassle (e.g. squabbling children) as well as the physical effort that must be spent in dealing with the hassle (e.g. bribing them with sweets or just cuffing them round the ear). Because hassles prevent us from reaching our main goal (e.g. getting to work on time), they can produce negative consequences such as fatigue or bad mood.

HOW SCIENCE WORKS

1. **The problems of dodgy memory** – Most research on daily hassles has asked participants to assess the impact of hassles experienced over the previous month. The accuracy of such memories tends to vary according to the time interval involved. More recently researchers have started to overcome this problem by using a diary method where stressors and feelings are recorded on a daily basis.

2. **Correlations don't show causal relationships** – Even when memories are reliable, the data they produce are only correlational. This means that we can't draw causal conclusions between daily hassles and our physical and psychological wellbeing. However, correlations do suggest that hassles have the potential to have adverse effects on our wellbeing, therefore we would be wise to take them seriously.

m ... dropped iPod ... missed bus ... out of-phone credit ... torn

THE TYPE A PERSONALITY

Friedman and Rosenman (1960) described the Type A personality as possessing three major characteristics:

- competitiveness and achievement striving
- impatience and time urgency
- hostility and aggressiveness.

These characteristics are believed to lead to raised blood pressure and an increase in levels of stress hormones, both of which are linked to ill health, particularly coronary heart disease (CHD).

The study – To test this, they conducted a natural experiment (to see whether Type A men were more likely to develop heart disease than men who weren't Type A).

They used an interview to assess the personality of 3000 men between the ages of 39 and 59. They also assessed the way the men responded to everyday pressures. As a result of the interviews, each man was classed as either Type A or B (i.e. showing no Type A characteristics).

personality

THE HARDY PERSONALITY

Kobasa and Maddi (1977) claim that some people are more resistant to the harmful effects of stress because they have a 'hardy personality'. This has three major characteristics:

- **Control** – Hardy people see themselves as being in control of their lives rather than being controlled by external factors.
- **Commitment** – Hardy people are involved with the world around them and have a strong sense of purpose.
- **Challenge** – Life challenges are problems to be overcome rather than stressors.

The study – Kobasa (1979) determined the stress scores of 800 business executives using Holmes and Rahe's Social Readjustment Rating Scale (SRRS). She assessed hardiness using a hardiness test.

Results - 8½ years later, twice as many of those with Type A personalities had died of cardiovascular problems than those who were not classified as Type A.
The Type A men also had higher blood pressure and higher levels of cholesterol: indicators of coronary heart disease.

Validity? Ragland and Brand (1988) carried out a follow-up study of Friedman and Roseman's participants 22 years after the start of the study. They found 15% of the men had died of heart disease, but found no relationship between Type A personality and death from CHD, challenging the claim that Type A personality was a significant risk factor.

Other research - Myrtek (2001) carried out a meta-analysis of 35 studies and found an association between CHD and only one component on the Type A personality – hostility. There was no evidence of an association between CHD and other components of the Type A personality.

and stress

EVALUATION

Research supporting hardiness as a buffer against stress - Maddi *et al.* (1987) measured hardiness in employees of a US company that was dramatically reducing its workforce over a period of one year. They found that two-thirds of the employees suffered stress-related illness over the year, but the other third thrived. Those who thrived during this period showed evidence of the three components of the hardy personality.

Negative affectivity (NA) may be a simpler explanation than hardiness. Individuals with high NA dwell more on their failures and on negative aspects of themselves and their world. They are also more likely to report dissatisfaction and distress.

Problems of measurement – Much of the support for the hardy personality has relied upon data from s elf-report questionnaires. These are criticised because people may exaggerate their symptoms of stress in order to make their situation seem worse, or under-report the severity of their symptoms in order to minimise their problems.

Results - 150 of the executives were classified as experiencing high levels of stress. However, they differed in their illness record over the same period. Those scoring a low level of illness tended to score high on all three characteristics of the hardy personality and vice versa.

Approaches to coping: *Problem-focused coping*

Common strategies include:

- Taking control of a situation rather than avoiding it.
- Evaluating the pros and cons of different options for dealing with a stressor (which will work best?).
- Suppressing competing activities that might interfere with our ability to deal with the problem.

Problem-focused coping is the more effective coping strategy provided that the stressor is *controllable* (i.e. there is a realistic chance of changing those aspects of the situation that are causing stress).

coping with stress

COPING WITH EXAMS
Folkman and Lazarus (1985) studied coping responses used by students. In the run-up to exams, problem-focused coping was more evident, with emotion-focused coping used more during the wait for results.

Emotion-focused coping

Common strategies include:

- Denial (pretending something isn't happening) and distancing (not thinking about it).
- Focusing on and venting emotions (crying or getting angry).
- Wishful thinking (dwelling on what might have been).

People typically use emotion-focused coping with those stressors perceived as less controllable. Emotion-focused coping can reduce physiological arousal levels prior to the use of a more constructive, problem-focused approach.

Gender differences in approaches to coping

Research has often found that females are more likely to use emotion-focused coping and males problem-focused coping, but why is this?

- **Socialisation theory** suggests that females are taught to express their emotions more openly, whereas males are taught to approach stressful situations in a more active, problem-focused manner.

- **Role constraint theory** explains gender differences in coping as a product of the *roles* that males and females tend to occupy.

Rosario *et al.* (1988) found that males and females in the *same* roles tended not to differ in their reported use of problem- or emotion-focused coping. This appears to support the role constraint explanation rather than a socialisation explanation for differences in the choice of coping strategy.

Research evidence

Penley *et al.* (2002) conducted a correlational analysis and showed that the use of problem-focused coping was positively correlated with overall health outcomes. Negative emotion-focused coping, on the other hand (such as the use of anger and avoidance) was related to poor overall health outcomes.

Rukholm and Viverais (1993) found that if a person feels a significant degree of stress when confronted by a stressor, they may first need to use emotion-focused coping to deal with the anxiety before then using problem-focused coping when their anxiety is under control.

Problems of measurement – The standard measurement instrument in research in this area is the *Ways of Coping* measure. However many of the items in this measure are more appropriate to coping with *some* types of stressor (e.g. relationship stressors) than others (e.g. health problems).

Is emotion-focused coping always maladaptive? – Emotion-focused coping may be unhelpful when dealing with certain stressors, for example it may prevent a person from seeking appropriate treatment when they are ill. However it can be useful during any recovery period, though it can distract the individual from making any necessary lifestyle changes.

Jargon watch

Problem-focused coping involves the use of strategies designed directly to deal with the stressful situation (e.g. finding a solution or seeking help).

Emotion-focused coping involves the use of strategies that deal only with the emotional distress associated with stressful events rather than the problem itself.

Emotion-focused coping is a passive process that merely changes the emotions associated with a stressor, whereas problem-focused coping involves taking direct action to solve the problem.

94–95

96–97

100–101

98–99

Social Psychology

Why do we conform?

Human beings conform for many different reasons - sometimes just because they want to be accepted, or maybe because they aren't sure of the best course of action.

NORMATIVE SOCIAL INFLUENCE

This happens when an individual agrees with or acts in the same way as the majority without actually *accepting* their point of view. It is conformity in action alone and is also known as compliance. Because humans are a social species, they have a strong desire to be accepted and a fear of rejection. This makes it difficult for them to deviate from the majority, because of the possible risk of rejection. This fear forms the basis of normative social influence. Of course, another reason why we just follow the crowd is laziness...

*Big fish in a little pond...*The power of normative influence has been demonstrated in a study by Garandeau and Cillessen (2006). They showed how children with a low level of friendships can be manipulated by a skilful bully so that victimising another child provides the group with a common goal. It also puts pressure on group members to comply to maintain the friendship of the other members of the group.

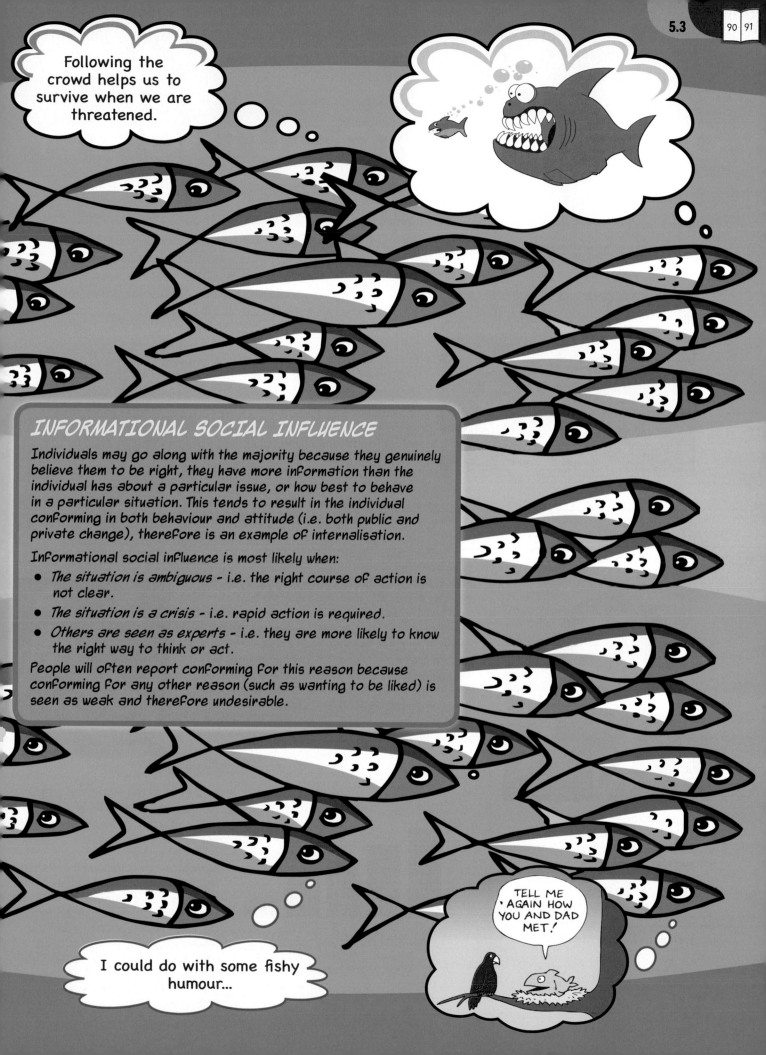

INFORMATIONAL SOCIAL INFLUENCE

Individuals may go along with the majority because they genuinely believe them to be right, they have more information than the individual has about a particular issue, or how best to behave in a particular situation. This tends to result in the individual conforming in both behaviour and attitude (i.e. both public and private change), therefore is an example of internalisation.

Informational social influence is most likely when:

- *The situation is ambiguous* - i.e. the right course of action is not clear.
- *The situation is a crisis* - i.e. rapid action is required.
- *Others are seen as experts* - i.e. they are more likely to know the right way to think or act.

People will often report conforming for this reason because conforming for any other reason (such as wanting to be liked) is seen as weak and therefore undesirable.

OBEDIENCE TO AUTHORITY

After gaining power in 1933, Adolf Hitler established a pyramidal power structure, with each layer of the pyramid required to show total blind obedience to their superiors in exchange for privileges and power. At the top of this pyramid was Hitler himself, under him were leaders such as Hermann Goering and Heinrich Himmler. Below them were the senior officers of the SS and so on. The Nazis' success, particularly their 'crusade' to rid Europe of all Jews and other 'unsuitable' groups, depended on unquestioning obedience to the cause at all times.

Social psychologist Stanley Milgram was interested in how apparently ordinary people could be coerced into carrying out such extraordinary acts because of the need to obey. To investigate this he carried out a lab experiment with 40 male volunteers, varying the situational pressures to see which had the greatest effect on obedience.

After drawing lots the real participant was assigned the role of 'teacher' and a confederate that of 'learner'. The teacher's job was to administrate a learning task and deliver 'electric shocks' to the learner if he got a question wrong. These began at 15 volts and increased in 15 volt increments to a maximum of 450 volts. Obedience was measured as the percentage of participants who went to the maximum shock level. All participants went to at least 300 volts, with only 12.5% stopping at that point, 65% continuing to the maximum 450 volts.

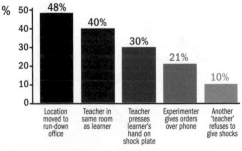

%

| 48% | 40% | 30% | 21% | 10% |

Location moved to run-down office | Teacher in same room as learner | Teacher presses learner's hand on shock plate | Experimenter gives orders over phone | Another 'teacher' refuses to give shocks

Maximum shock level administered

Variations to the study (see graph to left) showed that the proximity of the victim decreased obedience, as did the presence of disobedient allies. When two confederates refused to continue, almost all the real participants also withdrew, with only 10% continuing to 450 volts. When the experimenter left the room and gave orders over the telephone, participants felt better able to defy and obedience levels dropped to 21%.

When faced with a direct order from a figure in authority, a person has a choice whether they comply or not. Much of the work carried out by Stanley Milgram in the 1960s was to determine the situational factors which would compel individuals to suspend their own moral judgment in order to carry out the will of a more powerful authority figure. The impetus for his work was the defence offered by the majority of Nazi war criminals at the end of World War II that they had been 'only obeying orders'.

At the end of World War II, when many Nazi leaders were tried at Nuremberg, a common defence was that they 'were only obeying orders'. Under this defence, those individuals who had carried out the atrocities witnessed in the Holocaust claimed that as they were acting under orders, they were not responsible for their crimes. This 'only obeying orders' defence was rejected by the judges at Nuremberg, and consequently many of the defendants were sentenced to death for their crimes.

Ethics

Deception and lack of informed consent – Participants were told that the experiment was about the effects of punishment on learning rather than its true purpose. Consequently, they were denied the right to informed consent.

Right to withdraw – The use of 'prods' by the experimenter e.g. 'you have no other choice, you must go on' made it difficult for many participants to withdraw.

Protection from harm – Diana Baumrind (1964) claimed that participants were under great emotional strain, causing them psychological damage that could not be justified given the aims of the study.

Validity

Mandel (1998) argued that Milgram's conclusions about the situational determinants of obedience in situations such as the Holocaust are not borne out by real-life events, and quotes Browning's study of the mass killings carried out by Reserve Police Battalion 101 to support this assertion (Browning, 1992). For these men, situational factors such as physical proximity to their victims and an absent authority figure made no difference to their levels of obedience.

YOU WILL OBEY!

GRADUAL COMMITMENT

Milgram found that participants, once they had already committed themselves to giving lower level shocks, found it harder to resist the experimenter's instruction to give shocks at increasingly higher and higher levels. Stopping was made even more difficult because the transition from one shock level to another was very gradual (15-volt increments). Each shock was then only slightly higher than the previous one, an example of what psychologists call the 'foot in the door' approach. Once someone signals their willingness to agree to a small request, their ability to refuse larger requests from the same source diminishes.

AGENTIC SHIFT

Milgram argued that people shift back and forwards between an autonomous state, where they see themselves as responsible for their own actions, and an agentic state, where they see themselves merely as an agent for carrying out the instructions of another person. When they receive an order from someone in authority they shift from the former to the latter. Milgram believed that despite the differences in the situations, the process of agentic shift could explain the behaviour of his participants and the Nazi killers during the Holocaust, who claimed they were 'only obeying orders'.

THE ROLE OF BUFFERS

In Milgram's base-line study, the 'teacher' and 'learner' were in separate rooms, therefore when the teacher delivered an electric shock they did not have to witness its consequences. Buffers such as physical distance therefore protect the individual from at least some of the distress they may otherwise experience when they carry out actions that harm another person. The same is true in warfare, where soldiers have always found it harder to kill their enemy during close combat than when killing 'remotely'.

Evaluating the explanations

Gradual commitment – Robert Lifton (1986) found evidence of gradual commitment among Nazi doctors, who were first required to carry out sterilisations of those considered mentally defective, and then to carry out more and more extreme experiments in death camps such as Auschwitz. Insights from Milgram's research can help us understand some of the abusive behaviour of guards at the Abu Ghraib prison in Iraq. For example, the prisoner abuses observed in Abu Ghraib were also gradual in nature, coupled with the presence of compliant peers and an apparently unconcerned authority figure.

Agentic shift – Milgram argued that people would commit atrocities if required to do so by an authority figure. Mandel suggests that it is inappropriate to explain the findings from Milgram's study and real life atrocities in the same way. Holocaust perpetrators carried out their duties over years, yet Milgram's participants were involved for just half an hour. There is also a difference in their perception of harm doing, with Holocaust perpetrators *knowing* they were causing harm, whereas Milgram's participants were assured there would be no permanent damage.

The role of buffers – Milgram claimed that decreasing the physical distance between perpetrator and victim would make it harder to obey an order to harm the victim. This is not always the case in real life. Browning's analysis of the actions of Reserve Police Battalion 101 found that for these men, close physical proximity to their victims made no difference to their ability to carry out their orders to shoot innocent Jews at close quarters.

resisting social influence

It just wouldn't be right

In his study of conformity, Asch showed that some people would conform to a majority position even though they knew it was wrong. For Asch's participants the costs of conforming were not particularly great given the insignificance of the task, but the benefits were significant (not looking foolish in front of other people). However, if the task involved a moral dimension (e.g. joining others in cheating), there was less evidence of conformity as the costs (guilt etc.) were judged to be significantly greater.

RESISTING CONFORMITY

Its good to have a friend...

Asch also discovered that the introduction of an ally who also went against the majority caused conformity rates to drop significantly, but why? A fellow dissenter provides the individual with an assessment of reality, making them more confident in their own decision, and more confident in their ability to reject the majority decision.

Conformity levels dropped even when the dissenter gave a different *wrong* answer. This suggests that it is breaking the group's consensus that is important in resisting pressures to conform.

Dare to be different

Some people hate to follow trends and are protective of their individuality. Asch discovered that many of the participants who responded to majority influence with independence (i.e. they persisted in giving the right answer rather than agreeing with the majority's wrong answer) tended to be less concerned with social norms.

Some people go one step further than this and are predisposed to react to majority influence by actively opposing the norm, *whatever* it was. They may be fully aware of the majority's views but their behaviour is simply motivated to oppose them, demonstrating a strong anti-conformity dimension to their personality.

BE A SUPERHERO!

IT'S TIME TO MAKE A STAND!

I *WILL* RESIST!

Jargon watch

Independent behaviour – Behaving in a way that shows freedom from any control or influence of other group members, i.e. resisting pressures to conform or to obey.

Social heroism – When faced with pressure to go along with others who are behaving inappropriately, or to obey an unjust order, an individual chooses to resist these attempts at influence regardless of what the consequences might be for them.

In his book 'The Lucifer Effect', Zimbardo argues that while most of us would bow to the demands of an unjust authority, there are others who feel able to resist *regardless* of the consequences. He describes these individuals as displaying social heroism (e.g. Nelson Mandela, jailed for opposing apartheid in South Africa or Rosa Parks, heroine of the American Civil Rights movement). He believes that a key factor in social heroism is stimulation of the heroic imagination: a way of thinking that makes it more likely that people will be able to resist an unjust authority figure or pressure to conform to anti-social group norms and will act 'heroically' when the time comes.

RESISTING OBEDIENCE

Status
When Milgram's study was moved from the prestigious setting of Yale University to a modest office in the commercial quarter, more participants felt able to resist the experimenter. This tells us that status of the authority figure and of the setting is a key factor in obedience and its resistance. However it is worth noting that this particular variation of Milgram's original study has never been replicated.

End shocks NOW!

It takes two (or three)
Resistance was also increased in the presence of disobedient confederates, who provided social support and so made it more likely that the individual felt able to resist pressures to obey. The important role played by disobedient models has been shown in acts of civil protest such as the suffragettes and anti-war protestors.

A question of morality
In Milgram's study, those who based their decisions on more advanced moral principles were more defiant, whereas those who obeyed the experimenter completely tended to reason at a less mature level of morality. This isn't the same as religious affiliation, as Milgram also found that Roman Catholics were more likely to obey than non-Catholics!

A STREAK OF INDEPENDENCE

Why are some people better able to retain their independence than others? The answer may have something to do with personality differences, with independent people more likely to see themselves as masters (or mistresses) of their own life rather than victims of the controlling influence of others.

ATTRIBUTIONAL STYLE

When people experience success or failure in what they do, they make causal attributions for these events. The consistency with which they make specific types of attributions determines their attributional style. Psychologists have identified three components in a person's attributional style.

÷ **Personal** (i.e. either *dispositional* or *situational*) – People may tend to see themselves as the cause of events (dispositional) or may attribute the cause of an event to external factors such as bad luck (situational).

÷ **Permanent** (i.e. either *stable* or *unstable*) – An individual may see the situation (e.g. failing an exam) as either changeable ("If I revise more I may pass next time") or unchangeable ("What's the point, I'll just fail again").

÷ **Pervasive** (i.e. either *global* or *local*) – An event may be seen as affecting *all* aspects of a person's life, or having a more restricted 'local' influence. Failing an exam may be seen as indicative of their worthlessness or just that they are no good at psychology (or maths or biology or French…).

POST FEB. 15 TO FEB. 28

RESEARCH EVIDENCE – LOCUS OF CONTROL

Are we becoming more external?

Twenge *et al.* (2004) carried out a meta-analysis on young Americans, and found that locus of control scores had become substantially more external between 1960 and 2002. The consequences of this trend are worrying, because high externality is also associated with decreased self-control, poor school achievement and depression.

What are the reasons for this trend?

The rise in social factors such as unemployment, divorce rate and an increase in violent crime over this period has led young people to see many aspects of their lives as beyond their control.

LOCUS OF CONTROL

People differ in their perception of the amount of personal control they have over their behaviour. We can measure this dimension of personality in terms of their 'locus of control'.

÷ People with an **internal locus of control** perceive themselves as having a great deal of personal control over their behaviour so take more responsibility for it. Things don't just happen, they are due to ability and effort. High internals are active seekers of information and rely less on the opinions of others, and so are better able to resist social influence.

÷ Those with an **external locus of control** tend to judge much of their behaviour as being caused by external influences (or even luck), therefore take less personal responsibility for it.

Are internals *more* successful?

Rotter (1966) claimed that because people high in internality took more responsibility for their actions, they would exhibit greater initiative, making them more effective and successful at work.

 Is this the case? Linz & Semykina (2005) found no relationship between locus of control and earnings for male employees, but did for females, with internals earning significantly more than externals.

RESEARCH EVIDENCE – ATTRIBUTIONAL STYLE

Cultural differences in attributional style

Anderson (1 999) measured attributional style, depression and loneliness in Chinese and American students. Chinese students accepted more responsibility for failures and less credit for successes than did US students. This relatively maladaptive attributional style was associated with higher scores for depression and loneliness in the Chinese students.

Where does a negative attributional style come from?

Students who were more rebellious at school were found to have experienced more negative experiences and had consequently developed a negative attributional style (Heaven *et al.*, 2005)

PSYCHOL

SOCIAL CHANGE THROUGH MINORITY INFLUENCE

for more on minority influence see pages 88-89.

Gandhi and the Satyagrahi

SOCIAL INFLUENCE CAN BE used as a force for social change. Gandhi's dissent against the British salt tax in India acted as the catalyst for widespread social reform, culminating in the British granting independence to India in 1947. The aim of Gandhi's followers, the *satyagrahi*, was to convert the British through non-violent protest. To accomplish this, they would suffer the anger of their opponent when necessary and would not retaliate to physical assaults or punishment. Gandhi believed it was contradictory to use violence to obtain peace.

Research has shown that minorities must be consistent if they are to prevail. Gandhi required the strictest adherence to the principles of satyagraha (non-violent protest) during the protest march against the salt tax. The consistency thus demonstrated attracted an increasing number of followers as their message was taken more seriously by the people they met over the 23-day march. Research has also demonstrated that the power of a minority position is strengthened (i.e. augmented), if they are seen as having little to gain and much to lose. The influence of the satyagrahi was *augmented* by their willingness to suffer without retaliation. No women were present on the march, because Gandhi took the view that the presence of women might deter the British from attacking the satyagrahi, and so lessen the augmentation effect.

TERRORISM AND MINORITY INFLUENCE

Kruglanski (2003) has argued that many acts o terrorism are intended to bring about social change through minority influence Terrorist acts attempt to bring about social change when open warfare is likel to fail (minorities tend to be relatively weak compared to the dominant majority) Justification for this view comes from the following observations:

- **Consistency an augmentation** – the influence of a minority is most effective when it is both consistent and augmented (i.e. continues to draw attention to its position despite penalties). The frequen suicide bombings in Afghanistan and Iraq are an example of consistency (they are frequent) and augmentation (members of the minority may die in achieving this).

- **Internalisation** – An effective minority may lead to the internalisation of the minority position Terrorism attempts to bring about social change by conveying the desperation of a minority group and their willingness to suffer fo their cause.

GY TIMES

CIVIL DISOBEDIENCE

rave women defy Nazi ower in the Rosenstrasse

ANY PEOPLE believed t it was impossible for inary Germans to resist Nazi dictatorship and the ortation and murder of s during the Holocaust. wever, a street protest in Rosenstrasse in Berlin icates not only that stance was possible, also that it could be cessful. Until early 1943, zi officials exempted Jews rried to German non-Jews n the so-called 'Final ution'. In late February that year, however, the tapo also arrested Jews ried to non-Jews. About 0 were locked up in a visional detention centre he heart of Berlin, prior eportation to the death ps. On hearing of the sts, their spouses, mostly en, hurried to the enstrasse and a protest e out. The women

who had gathered by the hundreds began to call out together in a chorus, "Give us our husbands back." They continued their protest day and night for a week, as the crowd grew larger day by day.

Despite threats by the Gestapo to open fire with machine guns, the brave women continued their protest. One woman described her feeling as a protester as one of incredible solidarity with those sharing her fate. Normally people were afraid to show dissent, but on the street they knew they were among friends, because they were risking death together. Joseph Goebbels, Nazi Party Director for Berlin, decided that the simplest way to end the protest was to release the Jews. The implications of this protest

are that mass, nonviolent acts of noncooperation by non-Jewish Germans might have slowed or even prevented the Nazi genocide of German Jews. The fact that such

Rosa Parks and the Civil Rights Movement

ROSA PARKS's refusal to obey an unjust law sparked America's Civil Rights movement in 1955. She was arrested for refusing to give up her seat in a segregated 'whites only' area on a bus in Montgomery, Alabama. This simple act of defiance sparked a chain of events that eventually led to desegregation throughout the United States.

Power depends on continuing obedience. If people refuse to obey, then this power crumbles. Social change can, therefore, be

achieved through disobedience. This confirms what Milgram discovered in his laboratory studies of obedience. When two confederates refused to obey the experimenter, 36 of the 40 participants also felt able to defy the authority figure. The important role of disobedient models such as Rosa Parks has been shown in many movements for social change, including the Civil Rights movement in the US, and the anti-Apartheid movement in South Africa.

protests were not more widespread was perhaps due to the fact that people were used to thinking that neither women, nor nonviolent actions, could be politically powerful.

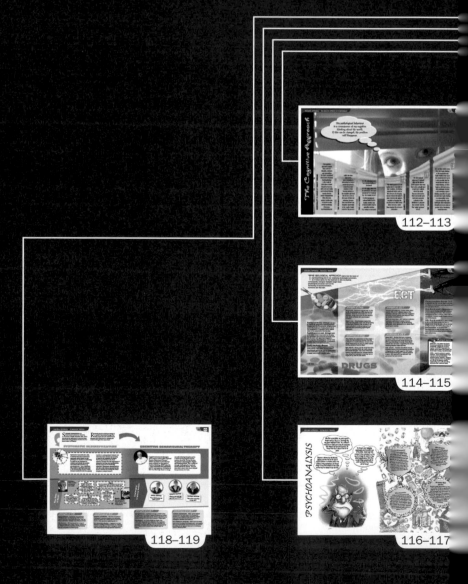

104–105

106–107

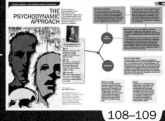

108–109

110–111

Individual Differences

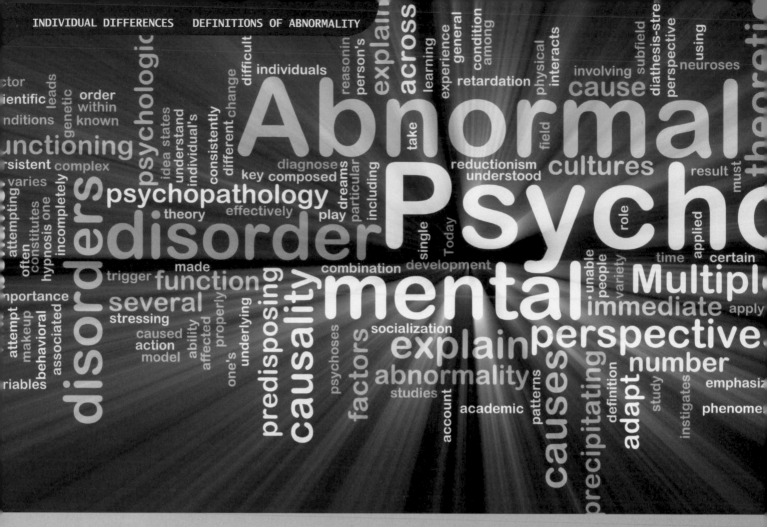

Defining abnormality

A ll societies have social norms – standards of acceptable behaviour such as politeness, appropriate sexual behaviour etc. These are not formal laws but implicit (i.e. unwritten) rules concerning what people expect in the behaviour of others. People who behave in a socially deviant way (that is, they display behaviour that *breaks* these unwritten rules) are considered antisocial or undesirable, therefore are *abnormal*, in the eyes of the rest of the group.

DEVIATION FROM SOCIAL NORMS

Limitations

Deviance is related to context and degree – Judgments of deviance are dependent on the *context* of a particular behaviour. Some behaviours are considered acceptable in one context but not in another. For example, urinating in a public toilet is normal, but would be considered abnormal if it happened in the middle of a shopping mall. There is also no clear line between what is an abnormal deviation (e.g. displaying antisocial behaviour disorder) and what is harmless eccentricity (e.g. wearing strange clothing).

Cultural relativism – Any attempt to define a behaviour as abnormal is pointless if we don't also consider the culture in which it occurs. What is considered a diagnosable disorder and therefore 'abnormal' in one culture might be considered acceptable and therefore 'normal' in another (e.g. talking to the dead is considered normal in some cultures). This means there are no universal standards for labeling a behaviour as abnormal.

DEVIATION FROM IDEAL MENTAL HEALTH

Abnormality is when a person deviates from an ideal of positive mental health, but what constitutes 'ideal' mental health? Marie Jahoda (1958) identified six characteristics that a mentally healthy person should possess. These include:

- *Self-attitudes* – possessing a positive self-esteem and a strong sense of identity.
- *Integration* – being able to deal with stressful events.
- Having an *accurate perception of reality*.

This definition proposes that the *absence* of these criteria indicates abnormality and therefore a potential mental disorder.

Jargon watch

Deviation from social norms– consistently acting in a way that most other people find inappropriate because it goes against generally agreed standards of behaviour.

Deviation from ideal mental health – acting in a way that other people regard as psychologically unhealthy or self-defeating.

Failure to function adequately – acting in a way that prevents the person from living a normal life and doing the things that most 'normal' people are able to do.

Limitations

Who can achieve all these criteria? – According to this definition, all of us are abnormal to some degree, as it is unusual to find people that satisfy all the criteria all of the time. For example, very few people have a positive self-esteem *all* of the time, and being able to cope successfully with all the stressful situations in one's life is clearly unrealistic. We might ask, therefore, *how many* of these need to be lacking before a person would be judged as abnormal?

Cultural relativism – Most, if not all the criteria of the ideal mental health definition are culture-bound, i.e. they apply to individuals living in Western cultures only. If we apply them to people from non-Western or even non-middle class social groups in Western cultures, we will probably find a higher incidence of abnormality. Some criteria, such as the criterion of *self-actualisation* (fulfilling one's full potential) are more relevant to members of individualist cultures than to members of collectivist cultures.

Mentally healthy people are able to operate within certain acceptable limits. If any aspect of their behaviour begins to interfere with their daily functioning (e.g. they avoid eating in front of other people or find it difficult to leave the house without checking and rechecking all the locks), then such behaviour may be considered abnormal.

FAILURE TO FUNCTION ADEQUATELY

Limitations

Adaptive or maladaptive? – Some behaviours that appear dysfunctional and abnormal may actually be adaptive and functional for the individual. For example, depression may lead to welcome extra attention from other people, which helps them deal with the stressor that initially led to their depression.

Cultural relativism – Definitions of adequate functioning are also related to cultural ideals of how life should be lived. This is likely to result in different diagnoses when this definition is applied to people from different cultures, as the standard of one culture is being used to measure another. This could explain why non-white individuals are more likely to be diagnosed with a mental disorder, because their non-traditional lifestyles are more likely to be judged as indicating a 'failure to function adequately'.

THE PSYCHODYNAMIC APPROACH

Freud's theory of psychoanalysis is the best known of the psychodynamic approaches to psychopathology. Freud believed that unconscious forces determined aspects of both normal *and* abnormal behaviour.

YOUR PERSONALITY BY SIGMUND FREUD

The Id
This is the irrational, primitive part of your personality. It demands immediate satisfaction and is ruled by the pleasure principle.

The Ego
The conscious, rational part of your personality, this develops because the young child must deal with the constraints of reality rather than immediate satisfaction of urges.

The Superego
This develops between the ages of three and six. It embodies the conscience and our sense of right and wrong, as well as notions of our ideal self.

What about ...
The Oedipal conflict

Young boys develop incestuous feelings for their mothers and rivalry with the father for her affections, which then leads to castration anxiety. Resolution of this conflict leads to the development of the superego, but in some cases the Oedipal conflict remains unresolved.

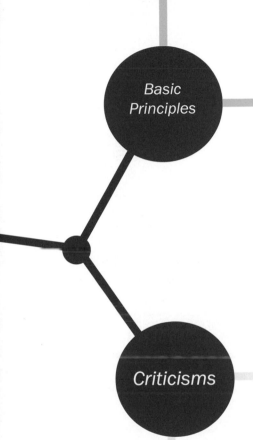

Unconscious motivation

The unconscious mind exerts a powerful effect on behaviour through the influence of emotions or trauma that have previously been repressed into the unconscious, yet continue to influence behaviour. This frequently leads to distress, as the person does not understand why they are acting in that particular way. The underlying problem cannot be controlled until it is brought into conscious awareness.

Early experiences cause mental disorders

In childhood, the ego is not yet mature enough to deal with significant trauma such as the loss of a parent and so this may lead to repression of any associated emotions in the unconscious. Later in life, further losses (e.g. divorce or redundancy) may release repressed memories of the earlier loss, causing it to be re-experienced and triggering a bout of depression.

Basic Principles

Mental disorders are *psychological* not physical

Freud's approach suggests that mental disorders such as schizophrenia or depression were not physical in origin but were the result of unresolved childhood conflicts (such as the Oedipal conflict).

Conflicts between the id, ego and superego create anxiety. This can be relieved by the use of ego defences such as repression (moving unpleasant thoughts into the unconscious), projection (blaming someone else for something the child cannot deal with) and regression (behaving like a child when faced with a difficult situation). A defence mechanism becomes pathological when it is overused and its use leads to significant problems in relationships and everyday functioning.

Criticisms

Lack of research support

The theory is difficult to prove or disprove scientifically, yet despite this difficulty, Fisher and Greenberg (1996) have reviewed over 2,500 experimental studies of Freudian hypotheses. They discovered that many of Freud's major claims actually did receive experimental support. Positive results were taken as supporting the hypotheses, but negative results were also frequently used as support for Freud's hypotheses. How come? Well, Freudians argue that if results go in the opposite direction to that expected, this indicates that the individual is using defence mechanisms to disguise the real underlying conflict.

Abstract concepts

Concepts such as the id, ego and superego are abstract (that is they don't refer to physical structures that can be seen and measured), so are difficult to define or to demonstrate through research. Also, because conflicts between these three aspects of the personality are thought to operate mostly at an unconscious level, there is no way to know for certain that they really are taking place.

Sexism

Freud's theory is undoubtedly sexually unbalanced (e.g. his emphasis on the Oedipal conflict in boys). This is not surprising given that Freud himself was male, and at the time in which he was writing, the cultural bias common in Victorian society meant that women were considered less significant than men. Nonetheless, this does limit the relevance of this approach to understanding the development of mental disorders in women.

Abnormal behaviours are learned

Abnormal behaviour is no different to other more 'normal' behaviours in terms of how it is acquired. If a behaviour leads to a desired outcome (operant conditioning) or is *seen* to lead to a desired outcome for someone else (social learning), then it is likely to be repeated. So, we can explain how apparently maladaptive behaviours such as panic attacks or anxiety get established, because they lead to something desirable for the individual (e.g. increased attention or extra support from those around them).

Behaviourists believe that normal *and* abnormal behaviours are acquired as a result of experiences that we have in life.

Abnormal behaviour can be adaptive

The environments in which behaviours are learned can reinforce maladaptive responses. For example, for an individual with agoraphobia, not leaving home lowers anxiety, which makes them feel better. Such behaviours may therefore be learned because they are adaptive for the individual struggling to cope with that situation.

Only behaviour is important

The behavioural approach focuses only on behaviours, i.e. the external, observable responses that a person makes to events in their environment. For example, someone with arachnophobia may display great anxiety in the presence of spiders. This extreme reaction to something that is essentially harmless is the abnormal behaviour that must then be treated.

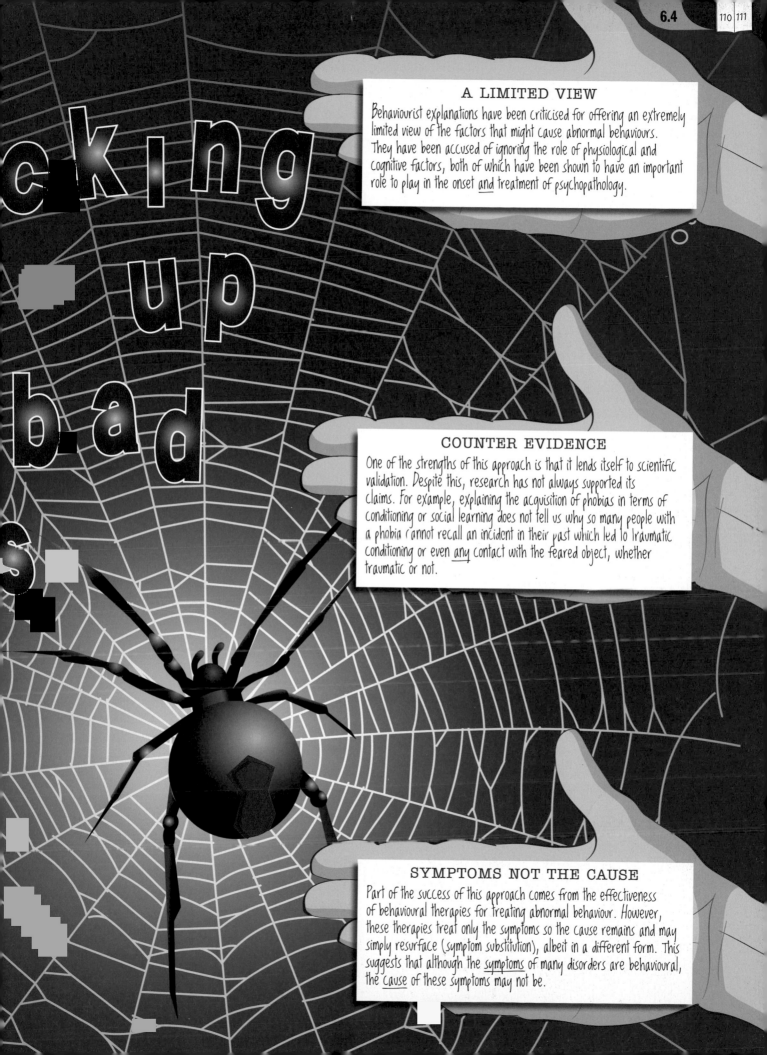

cking up bads

A LIMITED VIEW

Behaviourist explanations have been criticised for offering an extremely limited view of the factors that might cause abnormal behaviours. They have been accused of ignoring the role of physiological and cognitive factors, both of which have been shown to have an important role to play in the onset and treatment of psychopathology.

COUNTER EVIDENCE

One of the strengths of this approach is that it lends itself to scientific validation. Despite this, research has not always supported its claims. For example, explaining the acquisition of phobias in terms of conditioning or social learning does not tell us why so many people with a phobia cannot recall an incident in their past which led to traumatic conditioning or even any contact with the feared object, whether traumatic or not.

SYMPTOMS NOT THE CAUSE

Part of the success of this approach comes from the effectiveness of behavioural therapies for treating abnormal behaviour. However, these therapies treat only the symptoms so the cause remains and may simply resurface (symptom substitution), albeit in a different form. This suggests that although the symptoms of many disorders are behavioural, the cause of these symptoms may not be.

The Cognitive Approach

My pathological behaviour is a consequence of my negative thinking about the world. If this can be changed, the problem will disappear.

ABNORMALITY IS CAUSED BY FAULTY THINKING

The cognitive approach assumes that a person's thoughts, attitudes and expectations (i.e. their *cognitions*) direct their behaviour. Psychopathology is the result of distortions in these thought processes, with a person's faulty and irrational thinking causing them to behave maladaptively. When this goes against social norms or interferes with normal functioning, it becomes psychopathological.

THE PERSON IS IN CONTROL

Unlike the other approaches, where behaviour is determined by factors outside the person's control (e.g. their genetics or their learning history), in the cognitive approach the person is seen as the cause of their own behaviour, because they control their own thoughts. Abnormality is the result of faulty control of this process.

THE A-B-C MODEL

A is the <u>activating event</u> (e.g. someone looking at the house).

B is the <u>belief</u>, which may be rational (e.g. 'he is just passing by') or irrational (e.g. 'he is spying on me').

C is the <u>consequence</u> – rational beliefs lead to healthy emotions but irrational beliefs lead to unhealthy emotions (e.g. feelings of paranoia).

E

This model suggests it is the patient who is responsible for their condition, overlooking situational factors such as life stressors. By focusing only on events in the patient's mind, recovery only appears possible by changing the way the person thinks about these stressors, rather than changing the stressors themselves.

BLAMES THE PATIENT

E

Not all irrational beliefs are 'irrational'. Alloy and Abrahmson (1979) suggest that many depressives actually have a much more realistic view of the world than non-depressives. Depressed people gave much more accurate estimates of the likelihood of a disaster than 'normal' controls (the 'sadder but wiser' effect).

THE 'SADDER BUT WISER' EFFECT

E

It is not clear which comes first, the faulty thinking or the mental disorder. Faulty thinking may cause the mental disorder but it is also possible that the mental disorder leads to faulty thinking, as often happens with depression, when individuals develop a self-defeating style of thinking about life. It is also possible that faulty thinking is a vulnerability factor in psychopathology with individuals with maladaptive thought processes being at greater risk of developing mental disorders

IS FAULTY THINKING A CAUSE OR CONSEQUENCE?

THE BIOLOGICAL APPROACH claims that the cause of psychopathology lies in our underlying physiological processes, so it makes sense for the treatment to also be physical. Consequently, biological therapies target these physiological processes such as the functioning of neurotransmitters, hormones and the brain.

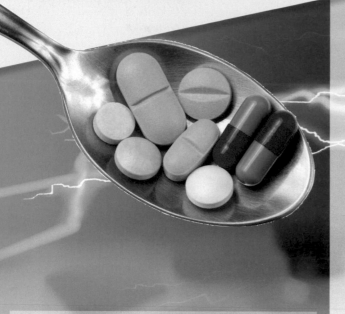

Antipsychotic drugs are used to combat the symptoms of serious psychotic illnesses such as schizophrenia. Antipsychotics used in the treatment of schizophrenia block the transmission of dopamine and so reduce many of the symptoms of this disorder.

Antidepressant drugs such as the SSRIs (think *Prozac*) work by blocking the mechanism that reabsorbs serotonin back into the nerve cell after it has triggered a nerve impulse. This prolongs its activity in the synapse and relieves symptoms of depression because of the increased stimulation.

Anti-anxiety drugs

Benzodiazepines reduce anxiety by slowing down activity of the central nervous system. Beta-blockers reduce the activity of adrenaline and noradrenaline (part of the body's response to stress) and so have a calming effect.

strengths of drugs

They work! – Research suggests that, on the whole, drug therapies are more effective than placebos. However, in the treatment of most disorders, drugs used alone are less effective than when combined with psychological therapies.

Easy to use – Drug therapies require little effort from the patient (other than remembering to take them), therefore they are likely to be more motivated to continue treatment than with more time-consuming psychological treatments.

weaknesses of drugs

They tackle the symptoms not the cause – Drugs only offer temporary freedom from the symptoms of a mental disorder. As soon as the patient stops taking the drug, its action ceases and the symptoms tend to return.

Side effects – Most, if not all, drugs have side effects, for example SSRIs can cause nausea and suicidal thoughts. This is one of the main reasons drug treatments fail, because patients stop taking their medication since they can no longer put up with the side-effects.

DRUGS

ECT

strengths of ECT

It works (sometimes) – Comer (2002) states that 60-70% of ECT patients improve after treatment, although critics have also suggested that 84% of these patients had relapsed within six months of receiving ECT.

ECT can save lives – ECT can be an effective treatment, particularly in cases of severe depression. As a result, it can be life saving, particularly when depression is so severe that it could lead to suicide.

weaknesses of ECT

Sham ECT – Studies that have compared the use of 'sham' ECT (no shock given) with real ECT have found that those receiving real ECT were more likely to recover. Some sham patients also recovered, suggesting that simply receiving attention helps recovery.

Side effects – Possible side effects include impaired memory and cardiovascular problems. A Department of Health report in 1999 found that for those receiving ECT over the previous 2 years, 30% reported it had left them with permanent fear and anxiety.

Electroconvulsive therapy (ECT) is generally used for severely **depressed** patients for whom psychotherapy and drug medication have proved ineffective.

How does it work? A small amount of electric current, lasting about half a second, is passed through the brain. This current is sufficient to produce a seizure, which affects the whole brain. Patients usually require between 3 and 15 treatments.

Why does it work? ECT causes changes in the way the brain works, but there is disagreement about the exact effects that lead to improvement. ECT affects the action of neurotransmitters, so recovery from depression may be due (at least in part) to improved communication between different parts of the brain.

Jargon watch

Sham ECT – the patient has exactly the same procedures as normal (e.g. anaesthetic, oxygen) but no shock is given. It is the ECT equivalent of a placebo and is used to test whether the shock itself is having a beneficial effect.

SSRIs – selective serotonin reuptake inhibitors. These antidepressant drugs only act on the neurotransmitter serotonin (hence 'selective'), stopping it being reabsorbed from the synapse so it can go on working, exciting neighbouring nerve cells and making the person feel a whole lot better.

PSYCHOANALYSIS

With **free association**, the patient expresses thoughts exactly as they occur, even though they may appear unimportant to them. This is intended to reveal areas of conflict and to bring into consciousness those memories that have been repressed. The therapist then helps to interpret them for the patient.

The therapist draws **tentative conclusions** about the possible cause of the problem. Patients might offer resistance to these conclusions (e.g. they may try to change the subject), or may display **transference**, where they recreate feelings associated with the conflict and transfer these feelings onto the therapist.

Behaviour is influenced by **unconscious desires** and fears that are the result of repressed memories or unresolved conflicts from childhood. During psychoanalysis, the therapist attempts to trace these influences to their origins and then helps the individual to deal with them.

Luka.

Length of treatment

A study of 450 patients by Tschuschke *et al.* (2007) found that psychodynamic therapies such as psychoanalysis were more effective over the long-term than they were over the short-term. The longer the psychotherapeutic treatments took, the better the outcomes were, indicating that it takes motivation and effort on the part of the patient for the treatment to be truly effective.

Effectiveness

An analysis of 10,000 patient histories estimated that 80% of these had benefitted from psychoanalysis compared to 60% who had received therapies based on different approaches (Bergin, 1971). This provides modest support for the effectiveness of psychoanalysis as a treatment for neurotic illnesses.

False memories

Critics of psychoanalysis claim that some therapists are not helping patients to recover *repressed* memories, but are instead unwittingly planting false memories of sexual abuse or even alien abduction. Psychoanalysts assume that a patient can accurately recall early memories that have been repressed but as yet there is little evidence to support this claim.

No better than placebo

Eysenck (1986) argued that the failure of Freudian therapy to significantly improve on spontaneous remission (getting better over time without any treatment at all) or placebo treatment, was proof of the inadequacy of psychoanalytic treatment. Eysenck points out that the success of behavioural therapies also casts doubts on the validity of psychoanalysis as a useful treatment.

Systematic desensitisation is a behavioural treatment in which the person is taught relaxation skills, and is then given the opportunity to practice these skills while being gradually introduced to the feared object or situation.

Rational-emotive behaviour therapy is a cognitive behavioural therapy that helps people deal with dysfunctional emotions and behaviours by changing the irrational thoughts that cause them.

SYSTEMATIC DESENSITISATION

Systematic desensitisation (SD) is derived from the behavioural approach, and is based on the principles of classical conditioning. It is used in the treatment of anxiety, particularly the anxiety associated with phobias (e.g. arachnophobia – fear of spiders). The patient is gradually exposed to the threatening situation under relaxed conditions until the anxiety reaction is extinguished. Patients can overcome their anxiety by learning to relax in the presence of stimuli that had previously made them anxious. Because the two responses of relaxation and fear are incompatible, the fear response is eventually dispelled. Systematic desensitisation can also work without presenting the feared stimulus but having the client imagine it (called 'covert').

How Does It Work?

Problem...
Patient is terrified every time she sees a spider.

Step 1
Patient is taught how to relax their muscles completely. (A relaxed state is incompatible with anxiety.)

Step 2
Therapist and patient together construct a desensitisation hierarchy – a series of imagined scenes, each one causing a little more anxiety than the previous one.

Step 3
Patient gradually works his/her way through desensitisation hierarchy, visualising each anxiety-evoking event while engaging in the competing relaxation response.

Step 4
Once the patient has mastered one step in the hierarchy (i.e. they can remain relaxed while imagining it), they are ready to move onto the next.

Step 5
Patient eventually masters the feared situation that caused them to seek help in the first place.

Result...
After SD, patient has overcome her fear of spiders and feels relaxed in their presence.

strengths of SD

Appropriateness – Systematic desensitisation is relatively quick and requires less effort on the patient's part than other psychotherapies. They are likely to persevere, making it more likely to succeed.

Effectiveness – SD is successful for a range of anxiety disorders such as fear of flying. Capafóns et al, (1998) found that aerophobics had less anxiety after SD compared to a control group.

weaknesses of SD

Symptom substitution – This form of treatment may *appear* to resolve a problem, but eliminating symptoms (rather than dealing with the *cause*) may result in other symptoms appearing later on.

Not universally effective – It appears to be less effective in treating anxieties that have an underlying adaptive component (e.g. fear of dangerous animals) than those acquired through personal experience.

COGNITIVE BEHAVIOURAL THERAPY

Cognitive behavioural therapies (CBT) such as Albert Ellis's 'Rational Emotive Behavioural Therapy' (REBT) are based on the idea that many problems are the result of irrational thinking. REBT helps the client understand this irrationality and the consequences of thinking in this way. This helps them to change any self-defeating thoughts and as a result become happier and less anxious about life. During therapy, the patient is encouraged to dispute self-defeating beliefs. This is achieved through challenging the irrational beliefs held by the patient. They are then able to move onto more rational interpretations of events.

Challenging irrational beliefs

LOGICAL DISPUTING

"Does thinking this way make sense?"

EMPIRICAL DISPUTING

"Where is the proof that this belief is accurate?"

PRAGMATIC DISPUTING

"How is this belief likely to help you?"

strengths of CBT

Appropriateness – A particular strength of REBT is that it's usefulness is not limited to people suffering from mental disorders, but is also useful for *non*-clinical populations (e.g. people suffering from examination anxiety or stage fright).

Effectiveness – In a meta-analysis by Engels *et al.*, (1993) REBT was shown to be effective in the treatment of a number of different types of disorder, including OCD (obsessive compulsive disorder) and agoraphobia (intense fear of being in public places where escape might be difficult).

weaknesses of CBT

Irrational environments – REBT cannot address environments that exist beyond the therapeutic situation (e.g. a bullying boss), and which continue to produce and reinforce irrational thoughts and maladaptive emotions and behaviour.

Not suitable for everybody – REBT does not always work and is not always what people want. Some people fail to put the principles they have learned into practice and others do not want the direct sort of challenging 'advice' offered by REBT.

Glossary/Index

C

capacity, in memory A measure of how much can be held in memory. Measured in terms of bits of information such as number of digits. 6, 7, 8

cardiovascular disorder Disorders of the heart or circulatory system, including hypertension (high blood pressure, and heart disease). 65, 68, 69, 74, 115

caregiver sensitivity 27

case study A research method that involves a detailed study of a single individual, institution or event. 30, 41, 50, 58

castration anxiety 108

CBT see *Cognitive Behavioural Therapy*

central executive Monitors and coordinates all other mental functions in the working memory model. 10, 11

central nervous system (CNS) Comprises the brain and the spinal cord. 82, 114

central tendency
see *measures of central tendency*

CHD see *coronary heart disease*

chemotherapy see *drugs*

children
attachment 22–37
day care 34–35
memory 15

Christmas 71

chronic stress 65, 67, 68, 69, 83

chunking Miller proposed that the capacity of STM can be enhanced by grouping sets of digits or letters into meaningful units or 'chunks'. 7, 8, 18

CI see *cognitive interview*

Civil Rights movement 97, 101

civil disobedience A group's refusal to obey a law because they believe the law is immoral. 88, 89

classical conditioning A new response (conditioned response, CR) is learned when a neutral stimulus (NS) is associated with an unconditioned stimulus (UCS). Initially, the UCS produced an unconditioned response (UCR). After learning, the NS becomes a conditioned stimulus (CS) which produces a CR. 22, 23, 118

clinical interview A form of unstructured or semi-structured interview, where the interviewer may start with a few prepared questions but further questions develop in response to the answers provided by the interviewee. Similar to the interview conducted when you consult your doctor. 49

closed question Question that has a range of answers from which respondents select one; produces quantitative data. 48, 57, 58

Code of Ethics and Conduct (BPS) 53

coding system A systematic method for recording observations in which individual behaviours are given a code for ease of recording. 46

cognitive approach to psychopathology Psychopathological behaviour is explained in terms of irrational and negative thinking about the world. If this faulty thinking can be changed, the problem will disappear. 112–113

cognitive approach
memory 6–19
stress management 80
therapy 80, 119

Cognitive Behavioural Therapy (CBT) A combination of cognitive therapy (to change maladaptive thoughts and beliefs) and behavioural therapy (to change behaviour in response to these thoughts and beliefs). 80, 119

Cognitive Interview (CI) A police technique for interviewing witnesses to a crime based on what psychologists have found out about memory. 16–17

cohort effect One group of participants (cohort) may have unique characteristics because of time- specific experiences during their development, such as being a child during the Second World War. This may act as an extraneous variable. 58, 59

collectivist culture Any culture which places more value on the 'collective' rather than the individual, and on interdependence rather than independence. The opposite is true of individualist culture. 29, 87, 105

compliance Going along with others to gain their approval or avoid their disapproval. This is a result of social comparison, which enables an individual to adjust their behaviour to that of the group. There is no change in the person's underlying attitude, only their public behaviour. 86, 89, 90

computer 7, 10

conclusions The implications drawn from a study: what the findings tell us about people in general rather than just about the particular participants in a study. 58

concurrent validity Establishing validity by comparing an existing method of measurement (e.g. test, questionnaire) with the one you are interested in. 49

conditioning Learning a new response. 22, 23, 111
see also *classical conditioning, operant conditioning*

conditioned response (CR) In classical conditioning, the response elicited by the conditioned stimulus i.e. a new association has been learned so that the neutral stimulus (NS) now produces the unconditioned response (UCR) which is now called the CR. 22

conditioned stimulus (CS) In classical conditioning, the neutral stimulus (NS) after it has been paired with the unconditioned stimulus. The NS now elicits the unconditioned response UCR, now called a conditioned response (CR). 22

confederate An individual in a study who is not a real participant and has been instructed how to behave by the investigator/experimenter. 59, 86, 92, 97, 101

confidentiality A participant's right to have personal information protected. The Data Protection Act makes confidentiality a legal right. 53, 58

conformity A form of social influence where people follow a position established by others. 86–91, 96
explanations 90–91
implications of research 98–99
resisting 96
see also *majority influence, minority influence*

consent see *informed consent, presumptive consent*

consonant syllables 6

contact comfort 23

content analysis A kind of observational study in which behaviour is observed indirectly in written or verbal material such as interviews, conversations, books, diaries or TV programmes. 51, 58

continuity hypothesis The view that there is a link between an infant's attachment relationship and later behaviour. 25

control The degree to which individuals perceive that they have control over important aspects of their life, such as deadlines, procedures, etc.
and abnormality 112
locus of control 99
stress 74, 75, 76, 78, 81

control condition/group The condition (in a repeated measures design) or group (in an independent groups design) that provides a baseline measure of behaviour without the experimental treatment (IV), so that the effect of the experimental treatment may be assessed. 58

controlled observation A form of investigation in which behaviour is observed but under controlled conditions, as opposed to a naturalistic observation. 47, 58

controls in research
experimental control 45
see *control condition/group*

conversion theory 89

coping strategies (stress) 78–79

coronary heart disease (CHD) Failure of blood vessels to supply adequate blood to the heart. 68, 74, 76, 77

correlation coefficient A number between –1 and +1 that tells us how closely the co-variables in a correlational analysis are related. 50, 59

correlational analysis Determines the extent of a relationship between two co-variables. 41, 46, 50–51, 58, 59
attachment research 34, 35
stress research 68, 71, 72, 73, 79

corticotrophin-releasing factor (CRF) is a neurotransmitter involved in the stress response. It is released by the hypothalamus and triggers production of ACTH in the pituitary gland. 65

cortisol A hormone released by the adrenal glands that is produced when an animal is stressed. 65, 66

co-variable A variable in a correlation analysis that is believed to vary systematically with another co-variable. 50

covert desensitisation 118

covert observation Observing people without their knowledge, e.g. using one-way mirrors. This is done because participants are likely to change their behaviour if they know they are being observed. 47

counterbalancing An experimental technique used to overcome order effects. Counterbalancing ensures that each condition is tested first or second in equal amounts. 46, 58

CRF see *corticotrophin-releasing factor*

critical life events 70

critical period see *sensitive period*

cross-cultural study A kind of natural experiment in which the IV is different cultural practices and the DV is a behaviour such as attachment. This enables researchers to investigate the effects of culture/socialisation. 28, 59

cross-sectional study One group of participants of a young age are compared with another, older group of participants, with a view to finding out the influence of age on the behaviour in question. 59

cue-dependent forgetting 16

cultural variations in attachment 28–29

cultural relativism The view that ideas of normal and abnormal behaviour differ from culture to culture. 104 105

culture The rules, customs, morals and ways of interacting that bind together members of a society or some other collection of people. 24, 28–29

culture bias 29, 109

Czech twins 33

D

daily hassles Those frustrating, irritating everyday experiences that occur regularly in our work, home and personal life. Measured using the Hassles and Uplifts Scale. 71, 72–73

daily uplifts see *uplifts*

Darwin's theory of evolution 24

data analysis see *qualitative data analysis, quantitative data analysis*

Data Protection Act 53

day care A form of temporary care (i.e. not all day and night) not provided by parents. Usually takes place outside the home and includes childminding and day nurseries. 34–35, 60
effect on social development 34–35
implications of research 36–37
quality 37

death 70, 71, 72

UNIVERSITY PRESS

Great Clarendon Street, Oxford OX2 6DP

Oxford University Press is a department of the University of Oxford.
It furthers the University's objective of excellence in research,
scholarship,and education by publishing worldwide in

Oxford   New York

Auckland   Cape Town   Dar es Salaam   Hong Kong   Karachi
Kuala Lumpur   Madrid   Melbourne   Mexico City   Nairobi
New Delhi   Shanghai   Taipei   Toronto

With offices in

Argentina   Austria   Brazil   Chile   Czech Republic   France   Greece
Guatemala   Hungary   Italy   Japan   Poland   Portugal   Singapore
South Korea   Switzerland   Thailand   Turkey   Ukraine   Vietnam

Oxford is a registered trade mark of Oxford University Press
in the UK and in certain other countries

British Library Cataloguing in Publication Data

Data available

ISBN 978-1-85008-548-5

FD5485

10 9 8 7 6 5 4 3 2

Printed in Spain by Cayfosa Impresia Ibérica

Paper used in the production of this book is a natural, recyclable
product made from wood grown in sustainable forests. The
manufacturing process conforms to the environmental regulations of
the country of origin.

Acknowledgements

Editor: Helen Broadfield
Design and layout: Nigel Harriss
Cover design: Patricia Briggs
Illustrations: Nigel Dobbyn, Harry Venning, Janos Janter,
Pulsar Studio.

Picture acknowledgements

The publishers would like to thank the following for
permission to reproduce images in the book:

Cover image: Olivier Le Queinec, Chris Cardwell

123rf.com; pp 10, 12, 40, 44, 70, 78, 106; Mary Ainsworth
p27; ARC/deathcamps.org, p93; ©Bubbles-Jennie
Woodstock p16; ©Carlini Group p116; www.cartoonstock.
com, p19; ©Corbis, pp32, 74; DesktopNexus.com, p62;
FEMA p100; iStockphoto p81; courtesy Alexandra Milgram
pp 92, 93; ©Museum of London p88; NASA, pp 42, 67;
courtesy of the National Archives p88; Mike Cardwell, p75;
Matt Brooker, p94; Time & Life Pictures/Getty Images p23;
WikiMedia commons pp 92, 93, 100, 101, 108. Fotolia.com
for the remainder of the photographs and graphics.

Every effort has been made to contact copyright holders
of material used in this publication. If any copyright holder
has been overlooked, we will be pleased to make any
necessary arrangements.